A Guided Tour of
the Ice House

Acknowledgements

Many thanks to the editors of the following, where some of these poems first appeared: *The Yorkshire Post, Bridport Anthology 2005, Arvon International Poetry Competition Anthology 2006, If Books, All Of These Things Are True And Not True (Jerwood Arvon), I am twenty people (Enitharmon), Thomas Hardy Society Anthology 2009, New Forest Poetry Competition Anthology 2002, Wading Through Deep Water: The Parkinson's Anthology, The North, Smiths Knoll, Iota, The Interpreter's House, Mslexia, anon, Smoke, The Poetry Paper, Poetry News, Magma, Brontë Studies.*

'Mourning Bracelet' won first prize in the 2011 Brontë Society Literary Competition, 'In Another Life' won first prize in the 2007 Yorkshire Open Poetry Competition, 'The Lovers' won first prize in the 2005 Bridport Competition, 'Eucalyptus Lawn' was commended in the 2006 Arvon International Poetry Competition, 'Mothballs' and 'A Jewish Giant at Home with his Parents' were placed in the Ilkley Literature Festival Competition, 'Cut outs' in the Bedford Competition, 'Taking Your Time' in the Grey Hen Competition, 'Away' in the New Forest Competition and 'The Homecoming of Sir Thomas Wyatt' in the Yorkshire Open. 'Bockhampton' was a runner up in the 2009 Thomas Hardy Society Competition and 'Dads', 'After Dad Died' and 'My Mother Wears Sweaters in Summer' in the Mslexia Competition. 'Elizabeth's Diary: 1ˢᵗ September' was shortlisted for the Bridport.

A Guided Tour of
the Ice House

Carole Bromley

smith|doorstop

Published 2011 by
smith|doorstop books
The Poetry Business
Bank Street Arts
32-40 Bank Street
Sheffield S1 2DS
www.poetrybusiness.co.uk

ISBN 978-1-906613-31-0

British Library Cataloguing-in-Publication Data.
A catalogue record for this book is available from the
British Library.

Typeset by Utter
Printed and bound by CPI Group (UK) Ltd, Croydon, CR0 4YY
Cover design by Utter
Cover image: Lovers in a Wood by Moonlight,
John Atkinson Grimshaw
Author photo: Michael J Oakes Photography

smith|doorstop Books is a member of Inpress,
www.inpressbooks.co.uk. Distributed by Central Books Ltd.,
99 Wallis Road, London E9 5LN.

The Poetry Business receives financial support from
Arts Council England

Contents

For my family, with love

A Guided Tour of the Ice House

Please mind your heads, ladies and gents,
and button your coats. We will be underground
longer than you think. Surprisingly cold
under the earth with only the worms for company
and the stacked up blocks of ice from the lake
to keep you fresh. Remember when winter
was an adventure? Those sword fights
with icicles, the joy of smashing a frozen dyke?

While you're down here, adjust the lamp
on your head. Notice how, at the edges,
the ice turns soft and how, in the middle,
leaves are caught and mayflies and even
the tail-feathers of a swan. For winters
were hard back then and the men who
hacked ice from the ornamental lake
and dragged it here were starved with cold.

See that hole in the roof? That's where
they were lowered in, in a bucket
with their sheets like glass in their hands.
And over there, to your right, a passage
where they'd crawl – the master
preferred them to be unseen, for his guests
not to know how he kept the meat fresh,
the secret of his chilled desserts.

You might be wondering how the ice
has lasted all these years and why
you never noticed the ice house before,
only the fish-pond and the mausoleum,
the rose gardens and the maze.
You might be thinking too how odd it is
the secret passageway is sealed and why
there is no bucket hanging from the roof.

Unscheduled Halt

Midnight and a new moon. The train
had stopped at Lille. The town
slept, at least as far as I could see.

Phil had his head on my shoulder;
I remember wishing I was not so bony,
no-one had ever rested his head on me before.

And when they did, when my babies
nodded off, their fists open, trusting,
I would remember this glimpse of Lille.

The night pricked with stars.
A stopped train. Midnight. A new moon.

Skylight

Just me and the moon, after all.
Beside me, you. Sleeping like a baby.
A baby who's taken a swig from the nurse's bottle,
a drag on a stub end he found in the ash-tray
and is now spread-eagled, one knee raised.
You make sleep impossible.

Anyway how could I sleep tonight?
I lie in what's left of the bed
like a jigsaw piece in the wrong puzzle
and watch the stars who don't care
staring back from another millennium.
They've seen it all before.

Just me and the moon, after all.
He might be just a sliver of his former self
but he knows what he wants of me:
my faithful gaze, his own reflection
in my eyes that stare up at him
through the cold, uncurtained glass.

In Another Life

I would have liked to take you to Pyramid Lake.
If you went there you'd understand why.

It's something about the greenness.
All those different greens
upside down in the still blue water.

And the quiet. Never such quiet anywhere.
You could hear an Osprey's wings,
the needles dropping from the pines,
the sudden somersaults of fish.

And the smell of snow makes you test the air
like one of those fallow deer at the edge
of the lake, sensing danger.

I would have liked to sit with you on the driftwood
and just look until it grew dark
and a bear appeared perhaps
and we didn't move.

It's autumn and the colours
are more intense for a while
like lovers who are about to part.

I like to imagine you there in your green shirt
lighting a cigarette, the quick, brave flare of it in the dark.

The Lovers
after Magritte

It was all his idea. Let's do it he said,
grabbing two tablecloths. I followed him,
giggling. Nobody saw us leave.

I sat bolt upright in the car in that brown blouse,
he kept his eyes on the road. It was so hot,
and him in his brown suit and tie.

When we got to our favourite spot,
that valley where the steep sides slope
down to a little stream

we solemnly draped the white cloths
over our heads and posed
for an invisible photographer.

Once the veils were on the laughter stopped,
now we were a blind bridal couple
feeling our way.

Rooting, fumble-mouthed for dry kisses
under a white shroud. Not like kissing eyes closed.
It was more than that and stranger.

He was a stranger, I was a stranger.
We did not know ourselves. Apple-bobbing
arms behind our backs.

We discovered the shapes of our faces,
his nose elongated, my cheek bones sharpened,
his cleft chin shrunk.

We could have been children
dressing under the covers,
exploring the hidden folds of our flesh.

We had thought – if we'd thought at all –
in our rush to get there, we would tear off
the masks, then our clothes,

that we would scatter them in the stream as we ran.
Instead we created new bodies under the folds
and then silently, by mutual consent,

took them off and, not wanting to look
at our old selves,
drove back to town.

Man Bathing

I never had myself down
as a Peeping Tom but today,
glancing up from *Ariel*,
I find myself watching
a naked man bent
over a sink soaping
his dark head. I see this
through the vertical slats
of a blind and there is
something hypnotic about
the way he moves his arm,
that blurred arc of back,
the skilled swabbing
of skull with flannel.
How long they take,
these private ablutions,
and how oddly touching
that final drying with
a blue towel and then
the combing of wet hair
in a mirror to the side.
How vulnerable the flesh,
that curve of belly
with its shadow of groin,
and now the back retreating
from the steamed-up glass.

The Homecoming of Sir Thomas Wyatt

When Sir Thomas returned from Italy
bearing the sonnet his wife gave him a cold
welcome. She'd had a pinnyful of roundelays
and epics, of his naked foot stalking
in her chamber at all hours declaiming
Sir Patrick bloody Spens and now this.
She'd been hoping for chianti, one of those models
of the leaning tower or at least a decent bunch
of grapes. And he'd been so irritatingly cock-
a-hoop. Men are like that. Have to plant
their little flags. She didn't let on though,
just thought 'Oh well at least it's short', folded
her arms and gave him a look like Jack's mum
when he brought back that fistful of beans.

Bockhampton

Imagine Hardy's bride weekending
in these cramped rooms, toying with her fork
while his mother, grim-faced, warns the others –
Henry, Kate, Mary – not to marry but work
for their bread, house-building, school-marming,
whatever but not, not if they've any sense,
fall into the same trap she did.

The resentment in Emma's breast
not lost on those at the tea-table
politely picking at Jemima's cakes
while Hardy sucks the tea off his whiskers,
thinks he'll take the air before bed,
leaves her there, his disappointing little wife
the one 'ugly did not come near'.

Under a pear tree he'll write about Florence
whom he almost kissed, Mrs Henniker
whose hand he held, dainty Agnes, but not,
not yet Emma with her hats like collapsing
birthday cakes. Later, in stiff sheets under
that tight little roof, she'll lie awake plotting
the book that will make her name.

A Haworth Triptych

Charlotte Brontë Gets a Laptop

It's grand for those mornings
when you wake to the bullets ricocheting
off the church tower, the groans
of Branwell going cold turkey,
Emily's infuriating cough.

You draw back the curtains
and by the watery, graveyard light
check you've got the right cigar
for Rochester to smoke in the garden,
the exact number of fatalities
at Cowan Bridge, the legality
of Aunt Reed's last will and testament.

You're responsible for more than half
the hits on friendsreunited
and a quick check of your inbox
confirms your worst fears;
Mme Heger has put a stop to the emails.

You meant to tinker with chapter 38,
you're not happy with the ending,
but Keeper's howling in the scullery,
Tabitha's banging porridge pans,
Ann reaches for a spitoon
and through the kitchen door
come the unmistakable tones of that curate.

Mourning Bracelet

I wear my sisters round my wrist.
Loop over loop their twisted
hair chafes my skin as I write
here in the kitchen late at night;
who is it clears her throat before
the clock's strike at turn of stair,
whose the face in the copper pan?

Out of the gate for air, I run
and they're leaping now from stone
to stone. Down the cobbled lane
I fly in Anne's best cotton gloves,
the hob-nailed boots Emily loved.
Footsteps when there's no-one there,
just these twists of my sisters' hair.

Japan Dressing Box
      left to Branwell Brontë by his aunt, Elizabeth Branwell

Sometimes I reach for it in the night,
trace her initials with my finger,
curse myself for not filling it with brushes,
paints, all those folded-up dreams.

Her night cap's on the peg, her pattens
by the door; but this is all I have of her now,
a lacquered box, cracked where
I've opened it over and over.

Inside, an empty gin bottle, a phial
of laudanum, Mrs Robinson's portrait,
her dear letters in a ribbon, and here,
under a lock of mama's hair,
the poems I will never finish.

Reading James Schuyler

Silver day, how shall I polish you?
or rather 'Silver day/ how shall I polish you?',
the line break clicks in but if you start

thinking about it, the poetry
bursts like a soap bubble. You can buy
a machine to blow bubbles now;

the kids all walk straight past it,
bored. But the whole world
was reflected in that bubble, the whole

wobbling, fragile world. Polish.
My dad was a polisher. Saturdays
were Cardinal days. He'd get a blob

of pink wax out of the tin and rub it in.
Even at the end, the ingrained skill
was there. You'd have thought

they were just sharing the chores
but she'd given him that to do because
he was one of those ducks

that follow you for life.
Now she's older than he ever knew
and someone else is paid to do the cleaning.

I've got no duster
but I'm going to buff this silver day
till I can see my face in it.

My Mother Wears Sweaters in Summer

hates August because it's nearly winter,
keeps a weather eye on the longest day
after which it's downhill all the way
to Christmas, which she also hates
and holidays which, for us, were over
by Thursday when she'd invariably
pack up and head for home.

She said her happiest moment was
looking in the mirror, holding
my baby brother, wishing she could
freeze time. I must have been jumping
up and down in the background, doomed
to be seven for ever, gap-toothed,
skinny-legged, awkward.

She sits in the window all day,
watching the birds on the table
she said she'd never have, counting
the minutes till tea-time when she can draw
the curtains on the chestnut tree,
the stone wall and those spindly roses
she bought in a moment of optimism.

Sex Education, 1962

The first erotic book I ever read
was from Lowdham Library.
They had a limited selection
and, not knowing where to start,
I began bottom right at Z
and had made it as far as W –
there wasn't a lot to do in Lowdham,
I'd read most of PG Wodehouse.
A huge lady with a sausage dog was in the way
so I reached round her and chose
a book that has no doubt since been banned;
I don't remember the title, or the plot
but I know on the jacket it said
risky as well as risqué. O Level French
was still two years away so I was
none the wiser. I didn't learn any French
from the book though I did learn
a few things the French get up to
and quite a bit we hadn't covered in Biology,
and now I'm reading this book with you.

Elizabeth's Diary: 1st September

Played tennis. Won 6.2, 6.2
Germany invaded Poland

In a low-cut tennis dress,
a little out of breath,
she comes through the French doors
to find Wilfred
hunched over the wireless.

Curled almond leaves are falling
as the newsreader's voice
attaches itself to the racquet.
She pours herself lemon juice
from a cold blue jug.

Richard trundles his horse
across the lawn, Patricia
pelts him with windfalls.
In the kitchen Mrs Bloomfield
is making quince jam.

Suddenly, as the result of an accident ...

You came down to the river the next day
at Briggflatts, one mile downstream
from the rope bridge. You picked flowers.
The flood had receded, leaving silt
on the reeds. You knelt on the bank
and closed your eyes, wanting to feel
the cold water wash into your mouth,
your nose, wash into your lungs.
And that letting go, the darkness,
a last blur of harebells. You imagined him
coming to rest here, caught in these reeds.
You gathered a clump of them, heavy
and wet in your arms, rocking, rocking.

It's fifty years later. Now I hold them.
The reeds are brittle; one breaks in two.
I thought it was a moth caught
in the flap of the little cream envelope;
then I saw it was a papery petal
from a pressed flower. Inside,
dried meadow-sweet, the seeds ready
to burst, a field vetch still purple
and a single harebell so fragile
it would turn to powder if I touched it.
Then, on the back of the packet I see,
in your familiar hand-writing,
Picked by the River Rawthey, June 1955.

Fifties Kitchen

Same mangle. That blue collarless shirt
on the airing-rack. The glass-fronted cupboard,
the tiered cake-stand, the grey nets.

If I opened the door to the pantry
the round tin with the King on would still be
out of reach between the siphon of Flit
and the bottle of iodised blood purifier.

Any moment now Grandma will walk in
in her Sunday pinny. She'll tell us
it's her favourite day: a lie-in, no breakfast, no lunch,

then mid-afternoon she rinses six potatoes,
pats them dry and slices
in two directions with that broken-handled knife
and slides them into the bubbling oil.

On the window-sill even the wasps sing
in their raspberry-flavoured graves.

But it's time to move on. A buzzer will sound
if you try to climb over that red rope.

Mothballs

So, camphor's carcinogenic. I *was* right
about the mothballs that choked me in the
doorway. I thought the moths ate them,
that she tucked them into grandad's drawer
to tempt their toothless jaws from feasting
on his socks. I hated their slamming panic
at the lamp, the way they plummeted, leaving
that foul brown bloom on the pillowcase, my page,
the heel of my hand. The big, fat cigar one
that stumbled in after last orders was so obscene
I couldn't bring myself to hit it for fear
of the colour of its blood, that creature of the night
who would strip my clothing as I slept, leaving
only a row of buttons down my chest.

A Jewish Giant at Home with his Parents
after Diane Arbus

Ever wanted to eat your folks
like icing dolls off a wedding cake?

I could sweep them up like dust,
shake them onto the flower bed.

They keep the curtains closed all day
to stop the carpet fading;

they don't like my nose, my hair,
my enormous feet.

Mum keeps a roomful of toys
as if I might regress,

looks up at me sometimes
like I'm some kind of ogre,

while dad stands, hands in pockets,
looking at his shoes,

diminished, defeated,
not knowing where to start.

I want to stretch out my arms
and shake the foundations,

stride off in my seven league boots
and find a ten foot woman.

Cut Outs

All they did was have babies, laid out in two rows
on blue candlewick, odd numbers on the right,
even on the left.

They never lived alone – or not for long. A suitable match
could be found in Woman and Home – grinning
in Y-fronts or a Guernsey.

Important that he should be taller
and she looking up, adoring, or with one hand
on the Electrolux.

They didn't talk, rarely ventured out,
or asked the neighbours in. Just smiled
and waited for the babies.

I snipped them from Cow and Gate leaflets
till they got wise to me at the Village Institute, then it was
gran's knitting patterns,

ads for Ovaltine or Wright's Coal Tar Soap. They were clones
in their two-ply shawls or got up in blue jackets
and bobble-hats.

What did they dream of, these wives in the biscuit tin?
New World ovens, Triplex grates, Acme wringers?
Bourjois 'Evening in Paris'?

Or the man at the pillow end, who always sat
waiting in his Tudor Saloon, not meeting the eye
of the woman in the beige hand-knit?

One Afternoon by the Esk

It comes back like a print forming
in a sink in the dark, that afternoon
with grandma. She'd thought I might
go rowing while she snoozed in a deck chair.
It wasn't the boat or the oars or the way
the water slapped at the boards:
it was the lad with black hair who put out
a hand to help me in, and the jolt as I found out
aged twelve, or was it thirteen, what that felt like.
And all the way up the empty river
with willows either side and Ruswarp station
and the train steaming by to Whitby
and the lady at the tea-rooms
tipping out her pinny of crumbs
for the clamouring ducks, I wondered if
I'd dare go back to the landing stage
when my number was called.

A Man Thing

Such a peaceful pastime,
long hours of reflection
on a folding stool
beneath a green umbrella,
feet planted where hooves
have trodden. On either side
wet grass, cow parsley, solitude.

Or so I thought, until you
took me out in Brown's Bay
and taught me how to reel,
how to spot the fish
on the ultrasound screen.
No peace here, just a pulling
against God knows what,

the ugly creature struggling
from the depths of the sea,
drowning in air, his mouth torn.
And all the way back
above the motor that banging
from the box, your bloodied hands
giving it some throttle.

Auntie Joy

Chalk to mother's cheese.
For a while she was everything I didn't want to be,
then everything I did.

Big-boned, buck-toothed, loud,
she was what you see is what you get;
told it like it was

and sometimes it hurt and sometimes not.
She made a house out of a barn,
a barn out of a house.

At her place, nothing stayed still.
Walls came down, went up again,
only somewhere else.

With her we swam in the rain,
traced the source of the stream, leaving
a rock to show how far we'd got.

The Year You Moved Out

Everyone else in the road wore blue
but I went to the maroon school
where there was a spare place
and endured Paddy Cahill who slurred his words
and had dandruff on his gown
and shouted *gedout* if you breathed.

I had a tinny Benkson,
with Luxemburg after lights out,
and dreamt of the dentist's son
who never gave me a second glance
though I walked up and down
outside his house all afternoon.

We went to watch the Dave Clark Five
though I had German Measles, was told to cross over
if I saw anyone of childbearing age.
They decided I'd be friends with Zibber,
gave us cake, left us alone in the same room
like an arranged marriage.

I went to church out of sheer boredom
or to show off my new bright yellow mac,
those wineglass heels mum persuaded me into.
I sat for hours listening to *Rubber Soul*,
writing boys' names in nail-varnish
round the mirror. And I missed you.

Di

You're standing in the garden,
holding a rag-doll. There's a brown swing
behind you. The grass is brown,
even the roses.

You're on a horse. I think it's Judy.
In your hand the crop grandad bought.
You're smiling in black and white,
a gap between your teeth.

You're pushing a pram. A brown pram.
You're wearing a mini-skirt and boots.
Everything is in colour now: your face,
the sky, even the polka dots.

1955

I know I hate stewed apple, cold bananas and custard,
tapioca and Mrs Stainforth, that Lonnie Donegan
is top of the hit parade, that I like watching the Interludes,
that my dad has an office and a secretary who gives us
barley sugar sticks. I know I love my cocker spaniel pup
and that I will never want to be friends with the sort of girls
my mother would have over the doorstep, that my new sandals
are the colour of ripe conkers and have little flowers stamped
out of the toes, that I want to be a vet and that I'm scared
of spiders, of big boys with sticks and of jumping crackers.

I don't know how happy my mother is or whether Churchill
is still alive or how my father bought this house or why
Mark Stevenson chose me to be his girlfriend, or if it's true
that it's safe to eat hawthorn leaves. I don't know if grandma
misses us or how I'll cope when Miss Russling moves to Goole,
if dad really likes his new job or why Mr Johnson next door
won't let us wash the car in the drive. I don't know the Latin name
for Old Man's Beard, or why Mr Davey spits on the path. I don't know
what's wrong with bringing Sandra home or how mum can be sure
it was her who gave me worms, or which cheek to kiss people on.

Thomas

By the simple act of leaning
from my arms, he makes me
disappear. And come back at will,
and disappear again.

I watch his surprise,
an idea dawning, that chuckle.
Today he's a god,
where he goes I go too.

Later he'll bang a fist
on his reflection, eat his face
in a spoon and stand alone,
wondering who he is.

The Terminal Building

Already it's not Australia
though duty-free shops sell
coasters of aboriginal art,
didjeridus that would have to go
as hand luggage, giant frogs
that croak as we pass.

At the gate you hand me my laptop,
I touch your hair. We hug,
the little boy at playgroup
who never moved from the curtain
and the mother who didn't know
what to do in the empty house.

DIY

Don't fret about the damp patch
under the window; the baby won't mind.

She'll not bother her head
about the lagging in the roof-space.

The bare floorboards that bring
the sound of your footsteps

will do her just fine, that crack
in the ceiling will be her first pattern.

She won't lose any sleep over
the missing loft ladder,

the crazed toilet bowl, the stubborn cold tap,
that creosote spilling through the fence.

Listen. Already she outgrows her prison,
drums her heels against its walls,

turns turtle, butts her head, blinks,
opens and closes her mouth.

Sit down, pick up your guitar
and sing to her.

Language Acquisition

Josephine is learning meanings
hot, sharp, no.

She has no words of her own,
though she's working on *cat* and *banana*

I thought adjectives came later
pretty, dirty, clever

and that first she must label stuff
teddy, daddy, moon

but I don't say anything,
just move the teapot.

Desperate Measures

Only after they've been gone nine hours
do we begin to dance, me and Josephine
who, just this morning, was content
to rediscover the world of Croc, to sit
in her playpen solemnly turning pages.
Set free, she scampered after the cat
who was always just one paw ahead;
then pulled herself up on my leg,
let go and fell into its water-bowl.
Since lunch we've played the xylophone,
pressed the red nose of the plastic dog,
releasing the notes of Old MacDonald
into the sunlit room. Toast was of interest,
banana, puréed parsnip. We went out
to say hello to the lambs along Town Path,
stopped to watch a girl in red wellies
feeding the ducks. Sleep did not appeal.
Now it's desperate measures, dancing
to Venus in Blue Jeans across the kitchen tiles.

Sleepwalker
for Jemima

Your arms reach out
into nothing. Your unused
hands, like new

rubber gloves have not felt
anything. Yet they know
the gesture that pleads

Don't leave me –
the bones of your inner ear
tuned to my heart,

my voice, my footstep.
Suspended on a thread,
Christmas tree angel

with seaweed hair, my nose,
your great grandma's expression.
I paint you, little mute mermaid

and already, on tiptoe
in the colourless dark,
you summon me.

Taking Your Time
(for Matilda Sakura Mullen b 14th March, 2010)

You didn't come on Tuesday the 2nd
when the poem on my calendar
was 'Kites', or on the 3rd when
it was 'Flowers'. On the 4th even
Alexander Pope couldn't tempt you.
By the 5th I was flipping over the sheets
barely reading the words. On the 6th
I didn't even glance at it, though I find,
turning over a week's worth, it was
a lovely piece called 'Scumbling',
on the 7th something about the human
condition I wouldn't want to greet you with
and on the 8th, by which time your mother
was in despair and not a twinge
to her name, I failed to read the one
about the elevator operator in Virginia
though it's lovely and I can almost
hear her repeating *third floor- men's wear,*
mezzanine. On the 9th, a week after
your due date, I read them, ending with 'Song'
Love laid his sleepless head
on a thorny rosy bed. By then none
of us were sleeping so, on the 10th
'Bad Blood' made me cry and next day
I was floating on the Sea of the Hebrides
like Fulva that can't be reached any more
and thinking of you and how close you are
and also how far away. On the 12th I flicked
over a prose poem about marriage,
my mind being on other things

and now on the 13th here I sit still waiting
for news, reading *You, my seedling,*
my days, my law. All promise lies with you
and thinking how already your mum and dad
who have yet to set eyes on you but
you're coming, you're coming, know that.

Paddling at Dickson Pool with Billy

You held my hand and tested the water with one foot,
then led me down the one two three steps
into the pool where children basked like seals,
threw bright balls or crouched to find out
where the sparkles came from. We followed,
step by careful step, the line of blue tiles to the shady end,
climbed out and ran to the slide, stopping to count
our footprints, to make them again backwards,
to fit yours into mine and dark they were those imprints
of your feet on land before they faded to nothing
leaving you climbing five six steps to be king of the castle,
to come down through the bridge of my legs,
braving the nippers of my fingers. Again and again
we did it, that game that went on and on in the sunshine,
the one two three steps, the slow walk, you leading the way
down the row of blue tiles to the sunny end and back,
examining our footprints, running to the slide and down
past the nippers through the bridge of my legs and back again.
The game that went on and on without question,
same actions repeated in the same order till they called your name,
strapped on a flotation aid, led you away for your lesson.

Afternoon with Billy

I don't know why houses in England
have stairs, sweetheart, but if they didn't
we wouldn't be able to go to bed.

I don't know why our spiders are small and brown
and you don't have to panic
or hit them with a broom

or why Meg died, or why we were cross
when she stole the butter
or why I said daddy tapped her on the nose.

I don't know why there are no birds today,
usually there are some. If we buy some seeds
maybe they'll come back.

I don't know why the frog came in
and hid under the table or why
I had to put gloves on to pick him up,

there's just something about frogs,
the feel of them, the way
all of a sudden they leap.

It's like you and snakes. At the zoo
you can look at them with only the glass
between and they're beautiful

but remember the time
a Copperhead reared up at you
on the path through the wetlands

and you dropped your scooter and ran
and the snake was trapped
and daddy daren't go past it to cuddle you?

Dads

They knew about watches and bicycles
and polishing shoes, about drawing a fire
with a sheet of newspaper.

Good at framing pictures
with passe-partout and worming cats
and opening up drains with a lever,

expert at tuning the wireless,
and pulling the TV aerial out
when there was lightning,

knew all about wasps' nests and beeswax
and how to deal with head-lice
and the best place to bury a hamster.

King Dick at catching spiders
in an upside down glass, button-
hooking a doll's arms.

Lighting rockets in milk bottles?
No problem. Could tell you what the voices
were singing in the telegraph wires.

They knew about the patients
at the de la Pole Hospital,
why they could never go home

but they did not know what to say
when the boy who said you were beautiful
no longer wanted to know.

Weather House

The couple in the weather house go in and out and in and out;
they've nothing left to talk about.

The lady with the parasol will never put her toe outside
on wet days. If she can't decide

she hovers in the doorway while the gentleman in welly boots
cannot stand the sun and shoots

indoors when she appears and doesn't even stop to greet her;
is that any way to treat her?

But she's as bad and cuts him dead, she never smiles or says hello.
I wonder was it always so?

Or did they once upon a time hold hands and venture out together
and never talk about the weather?

Away

Back home my father's having a brain scan.
He's afraid they'll find something
and lock him up. I'm admiring a view
in Umbria, looking out over tiles
shaped like hotel curls of butter.

I've left that other me behind. They say
it could arrive any day. Domani perhaps,
or dopodomani. The airline has a new scam
to cut costs. It leaves your luggage at Stansted.
Surely it should be enough to deposit you
beside a pool with what you stand up in,
a passport, a few hundred euro,
a breeze in the olive grove, a lizard on a wall?

The sky is every different shade of blue,
white almost, where it meets the mountains
I can't photograph. I have no palette
to mix the greens of cedar, bay and almond,
no fine tip to trace a criss-cross orchard,
that avenue of cypress leading to a farm.

They'll be sliding my father out now
from a machine like a mortuary drawer.
They'll unhinge his visor, let him go,
then start to examine the tell-tale gaps
where memories were; the pier at Saltburn,
the cliff-lift, the way we pressed our noses
on the glass to watch the sea rise
to meet us, slate-grey edged with white.

The Last Time

The last time I saw my father
he was sitting at a formica table
with two shop-window dummies.
All three were wearing blue plastic bibs
and a nurse in a sweater was spooning in
rice pudding and strawberry jam.
Like one of those tea-parties for dolls.
You'd prop them up on chairs and tell them
to be good. They never picked up
the cutlery, or spoke, or swallowed
a mouthful of the biscuit and water pudding.
In the end you'd drift outdoors to play
and, for weeks, picked bits of food
from nostrils, ears, tight rosebud mouths
and the dolly cardigans grandma made.

South Bank and Eston Rotary Club, 1951

I don't spot him at first, just Rhett Butler
at the front, next to a chap with big ears
and a down-the-rabbit-hole watch chain,
and some dude with a handlebar moustache,
but he's there from the neck up in the last row
between Mr Bean and Bart Simpson. My dad.
How long since I knew him, this young man
in specs, black hair thinning, that domed head.

How proud he is to have made it to this ballroom.
He even kept the menu. Oh dad, did you bring me
the mint or one of those Fraises Romanoff?
I must have been keeping myself awake, listening
for the scrape of your handlebars on the wall,
the familiar tic-tic of your dynamo.

The Morning My Father Died

Our guest was having a bath;
I was making the table look pretty-
warm croissants in a basket,
fresh orange in a jug, a white dish
with a spoonful of marmalade.

My mother's voice on the phone, quite normal
I think your father may have gone
She'd had a phone-call of her own,
couldn't make any sense of it,
thought she'd better warn me.

I went back into the room and Tom
was helping himself to butter and jam.
I asked if he wanted coffee or tea,
hesitated to interrupt
his conversation with my daughter.

I warmed the cafetière – the big one
that makes eight cups if you fill it full,
put four scoops in, lowered the lid,
poured milk into the best green jug.
I think my father may have died,

I said, as if trying out the words,
I couldn't remember whether you take sugar.
The talking stopped. They looked at me.
I swept some pastry crumbs up with my hand,
slowly pushed down the plunger.

The First Time

I thought I'd never wake
from the horror of his despair,

the second I found him rattling the locks
of the French windows;

he didn't know about the bolt
I'd had fitted since he died

and, turning, fell on me, too heavy
to support so I staggered

like a clown dancing
with a dummy fixed to his shoes.

The third time I went to collect him
and they wheeled out a barrow

with his body in it, slumped like a guy.
I knew then I had to lug it everywhere I went.

After Dad Died

She became that kid the teacher asked you
to look after, the one you played a trick on,
who wore a posh coat and was too scared
to balance along the water-pipe,
didn't see the point of worm-racing,
and had never set foot in a caravan
or owned a rat or lied her way into an A film
or borrowed her sister's nylons and sat
on that bench for a bet to count how many
lorry-drivers gave her a honk. The one
who wouldn't nick three-pence to buy chuddy,
or shout *Where's your boyfriend's shirt?*
at Sylvia with the fat arse, too chicken
to test the ice on the dyke or walk barefoot
through the ashes. The one on the edge
of the playground who was dying to go home.

Pilgrimage

The too bright polyanthus on your step,
the rusting wrought-iron gate,
a chip paper blown along the sand.
In the distance the steel works
a scribble on a grey sky.
A boy picking up sea-coal,
a cricket match through the arch
of your old school, a lad
with red hair, running, running.

And then the pram-faced town,
the boarded-up bookies
like neglected teeth
and the voices familiar, longed-for.
The almost forgotten accent I strain
to hear; a bill-board clattering.

Eucalyptus Lawn

Up a gum tree you said but which one?
There are so many and each with its neat label:
eucalyptus caliginosa, Bancroft's redgum, Scaly bark,
Argyle apple, river peppermint and Scribbly Gum.

I sit on a bench beside the Twiggy Daisy Bush
and look up at bone-white trunks
like a lover's legs glimpsed in the morning,
so beautiful you lie and watch them
grow whiter in the rumpled bed.

They are bare and humble under a blue sky.
Magpies warble from the tops. Brittle leaves fall.
A sound of water in a parched land.

And you, who used to say *up a gum tree*
never saw one, never sat alone with this yellow butterfly,
listening to the strangled cry of parrots.

How white, how like these tapering branches your limbs were
when you no longer left your bed and could not sip
the water you thirsted for.

Visitor

Eleven o'clock. An October Thursday.
Through the window, low sun
filtered by the apple tree.
Behind me the rocking chair,
the fire catches at last.
And he's there, I know it.
I don't need to turn,
just feel his presence.
I stay quite still, my hands
on the edge of the sink,
watching the sparrows
come down for cake crumbs.

'They came back, all the dolls'

Midnight. They rise from
their presentation boxes
with hard, painted smiles.

One walks stiff as a great aunt,
another lifts her posable arms,
the fairy doll rubs at the hole

in her hand, wailing for her wand
while the wee-wee doll
curls up with shame.

A naked Queenie opens
and closes her mouth. Mute
since I bathed her,

her drowned voice
mama, mama, mama,
one eye-socket empty.

The nursery-rhyme doll jerks
towards, the key in her back
spinning, mouth tight shut *Mary, Mary*

And what has my love done
to the sailor doll? His cracked
grin is terrible, his bitten off ear.

If I'd been Santa Claus

If I'd been Santa Claus
I wouldn't have lived in a semi
in a place in North Yorkshire;
I'd have set sail from
my fur-lined igloo once a year
over the whole sleeping world.

I'd have grown a wonderful beard,
slopped about in an old red dressing gown,
roaring my head off and left
a map of wet footprints.
My best friends would have been
Thunder and Lightning and Blizzard.

I wouldn't have met my kids
but spent the whole year alone
in my glittering ice-house imagining
the thing they most wanted
and leaving it for them
to find when they woke up.

I'd have met only the stars,
the moon and the velvet dark,
the owls, the bats, a curious fox
and the children of strangers
for one startled moment
before sleep claimed them.

If I'd been Santa Claus
there'd have been no
swanky play-stations,
no naff Disney spin-offs,
no carrots, no coal, no disappointment,
no wrinkled apple in the toe of a sock.

The Shortest Day

3.50 and already I'm closing out
the dark and the huge snow-flakes
that fall like ripped-up paper
on the parked cars, the rockery,
Mrs Next Door's red umbrella.
Two children pass with a sledge-
soundless and yet I can hear
the squeak of boots on packed snow.
Their dog, crazier than ever,
runs in circles barking at
the suddenness of it.
The half-closed curtain is rough
and warm to my touch. All colour
has gone in this darkened room;
the world has shrunk to a full moon,
snow under a street lamp,
that red umbrella. Years ago
we walked up a snowy hill
to a white front door and closed it
softly behind us. The room was cold
and the blue vase of narcissi
and the books and a little gold
Christmas tree watched us.

A Candle for Lesley

I lit a candle today, one of those night-lights
it's difficult to get a flame going on.
Felt a fool but had to do it anyway,
having gone in. January, and the Minster
emptied of chairs, the nave an echoing expanse
where school parties were shepherded
from Rose Window to roof bosses upside down
in a mirrored trolley. The whole of the East end
was a mass of scaffolding, workmen taking out
panes, shouting down to one another as if
they were fitting PVC. And me,
in the middle of it all, thinking of you.
Not praying exactly for how could I in that place?
You might as well try to be alone with God
in Newgate market, or the fruit and veg aisle
in Tesco's which was where I was standing
when you rang. You said you were not ready
and I said I should hope not, and afterwards
stood with my phone, my list, my half full basket.
A man reached across for bananas
while his wife steered round me and sighed.

Church

You waved away the guided tour,
side-stepped the welcomer. What you wanted

was to sit awhile in a beam of coloured light
just staring upwards. This church is like the one

you went to that night and found the vicar,
a dewdrop on his nose, digging a grave.

He said not to let the bats in,
wiped the mud from his hands

and followed you to the altar where you said
I do but it was only a rehearsal.

Stepping Out

My poor old legs
criss-crossed

by spidery red veins,
have walked how

many miles now
with you and how

many without,
yet you still say

they're lovely,
Here – you laugh –

it's this bit I love,
kissing me

in the exact spot
you know takes me

out of this room till
I'm striding, leggy,

twenty-one, towards you
in that dress.

Winding the Clocks

Each night you do the rounds, like a lover who
keeps faith after the loved one's gone;
I guess it's at the root of all you do.

I'm thinking this as you set the alarm,
lock the front door, hoist the pendulum; it falls to you
now to wind the grandfather in the hall, your arm

in the mahogany case your father loved, your blue
sleeve brushing the dust at the back,
your fingers round the heavy weight he knew.

Then you cross the room to mother's clock,
the one that once stood on the nursery shelf,
its soft chime still chides your dad for his lack

of punctuality. The grandfather strikes the half
hour, your brother's carriage clock an echo
from the breakfast room. All your life

cantankerous, out of step, yet still they go.
Listen. If the clocks bring back the way it used to be
and what it is you've lost, perhaps they know

what time still holds in store for you. And me.
Still here, watching you turn that small brass key.

Where I was

It was one of
those days when it was good
to be indoors, when just

sipping black tea from a spotted
cup was enough.
The news was hushed.

He didn't want to tell us;
once he'd said it
it would be real.

And afterwards, it snowed.
The whole window-frame
was filled with it. So soft,

each flake touched
the window, as if
it had never been.

Smith/Doorstop Books, Pamphlets and Audio

25years

of titles by

Moniza Alvi, Simon Armitage, Jane Aspinall, Ann Atkinson, Sally Baker, Mike Barlow, Kate Bass, Suzanne Batty, Chris Beckett, Catherine Benson, Gerard Benson, Sujata Bhatt, Nina Boyd, Sue Boyle, Susan Bright, Carole Bromley, Sue Butler, Liz Cashdan, Dennis Casling, Julia Casterton, Clare Chapman, Linda Chase, Debjani Chatterjee, Stanley Cook, Bob Cooper, Jennifer Copley, Paula Cunningham, Simon Currie, Duncan Curry, Peter Daniels, Jonathan Davidson, Kwame Dawes, Julia Deakin, Steve Dearden, Patricia Debney, Tim Dooley, Jane Draycott, Carol Ann Duffy, Sue Dymoke, Nell Farrell, Catherine Fisher, Janet Fisher, Sam Gardiner, Adele Geras, Sally Goldsmith, Yvonne Green, Harry Guest, Robert Hamberger, Sophie Hannah, John Harvey, Jo Haslam, Geoff Hattersley, Jeanette Hattersley, Marko Hautala, Selima Hill, Andrea Holland, Sian Hughes, Keith Jafrate, Lesley Jeffries, Chris Jones, Mimi Khalvati, John Killick, Stephen Knight, Judith Lal, John Lancaster, Peter Lane, Michael Laskey, Brenda Lealman, Tim Liardet, John Lyons, Cheryl Martin, Eleanor Maxted, Michael McCarthy, John McAuliffe, Patrick McGuinness, Kath Mckay, Paul McLoughlin, Hugh McMillan, Ian McMillan, Allison McVety, Hilary Menos, Paul Mills, Hubert Moore, David Morley, Paul Munden, Sean O'Brien, Padraig O'Morain, Les Murray, Stephanie Norgate, Christopher North, Dorothy Nimmo, Carita Nystrom, Alan Payne, Pascale Petit, Ann Pilling, Mike Di Placido, Jim Pollard, Simon Rae, Irene Rawnsley, Ed Reiss, Padraig Rooney, Jane Routh, Michael Schmidt, Myra Schneider, Ted Schofield, Kathryn Simmonds, Lemn Sissay, Felicity Skelton, Catherine Smith, Elspeth Smith, Joan Jobe Smith, Cherry Smyth, Pauline Stainer, Martin Stannard, Adam Strickson, Mandy Sutter Diana Syder, Pam Thompson, Susan Utting, Steven Waling, Martyn Wiley, Andrew Wilson, River Wolton, Sue Wood, Anna Woodford, Mary Woodward, Cliff Yates …

www.poetrybusiness.co.uk